ONBOARDED
FOR MANAGERS

This publication is designed to provide accurate and authoritative information in regard to the subject matter covered at the time of publication. It is sold on the understanding that the publisher is not engaged in rendering professional services. If professional advice or other expert assistance is required regarding any subject matter covered in this book, the services of a competent professional should be sought.

Cover and book design by Tom Howey

For more information, address:
brad.giles@evolutionpartners.com.au

www.evolutionpartners.com.au

ONBOARDED FOR MANAGERS

*Helping managers bring new hires to the point
where they are effective, faster*

BRAD GILES

To my wife Maggie, and my children Mitchell, Reece, Cameron, and Amelie.
Thank you.

Contents

Introduction

You can't be held accountable for what you don't understand

For managers, it can sometimes feel like responsible humans are an endangered species. It seems so very hard to find people who take responsibility for the desired results. To be a manager is to manage people. And people are complicated, unlike the more technical or task-based work that many managers had experienced in previous roles. But managers must also understand that management is an entirely different job, and rather than your personal productivity, the key to success in previous roles, management is about your team's productivity. The success you experience, is in fact, only the success your team experiences.

I believe most people want to be successful in their job and most managers want their direct reports to succeed. I also believe misunderstanding is the greatest source of misery in the workplace today and the greatest opportunity we face.

This book, *Onboarded for Managers*, is an adjunct to my second book *Onboarded*. *Onboarded* was not written for HR thought leaders to pontificate about the HR process in university lecture halls. It was written for busy business owners and leaders to make a business case that onboarding debt costs more than you ever imagined. My research about onboarding was extensive. I surveyed more than 1,100 CEOs and hiring managers and interviewed fifteen leaders from across the globe. I wanted to understand what worked and didn't work for them. I also reviewed as many books, articles, and interviews about onboarding as I could find to get an aggregated view of the best practices. I'll share this research with you throughout this book. However, the detailed research version is contained in the *Onboarded* book.

In *Onboarded*, we heard the story of Nick and his boss Alex and Nick's frustration because he didn't understand how to succeed in his role. In this book, the roles are reversed, and we hear the story of Nick's boss Alex, who is frustrated because his team aren't taking responsibility and too many are quitting.

In my time in business, I've seen too many bosses like Alex lose promising employees like Nick. Over time, this has disastrous effects in terms of wasted resources, reduced productivity, and unrealised business outcomes – not to mention the stress and anguish it creates for both employees and managers.

I wrote this book because I don't want you to be like Nick's boss Alex. Instead, I want to equip you with the tools and knowledge you need to make your new hires valuable, productive, and effective team members – fast. By the end of this book, you will know exactly what to do to help each new hire succeed in their new role. You will comprehend the staggering cost of ineffective onboarding and how to fix it. This book will provide you with a practical and straightforward toolset to ensure your next hire has the best chance of succeeding. And if you've hired the wrong person, you will find out quickly and be able to act much faster.

I've been helping leadership teams build great companies for over a dozen years. Before that, I was an entrepreneur in one way or another for more than fifteen years. During this time, I learned that the first and most important rule of building a great company is getting the right people in the right seats and doing the right things in the right way. Everything else you want to achieve, any strategy, project, mission, or initiative, will struggle to succeed if you don't get that first rule right. And so, when hiring is done well, it should get the right people in the right seats. But onboarding is the missing piece of the puzzle. Onboarding takes those right people who are in the right seat from hiring and gets them to do the right things in the right way.

I also realised that the first rule of building a great company presents many important questions for leaders and that most of those questions are answered with effective onboarding. Over many years, this led me to develop and evolve a process to enable managers to confidently ensure that any new hire is the right person, in the right seat, doing the right things in the right way. I call this the onboarding sprint plan, and I'll take you through it later in this book.

The more I used the onboarding sprint plan with the teams I worked with, the clearer I became about the cost of ineffective onboarding in all its forms. I felt compelled to write this book to help leaders understand the actual cost of ineffective onboarding and share my simple process to overcome the problem – thereby positively impacting both leaders' and new hires' productivity and happiness.

In my first book, *Made to Thrive: The Five Roles to Evolve Beyond Your Leadership Comfort Zone*, I asked, "What's the difference between a good leader and a great leader?" In both *Onboarded* and this book, I ask, "How can we reduce onboarding debt and make new hires more effective, faster?"

The story within this book is a work of fiction. Any resemblance to real life is merely unavoidable.

Let's get started.

CHAPTER 1

The Candidate Whisperer

"There's this one guy—he's great, but I doubt we could get him," said Sarah as she pushed the pile of seven printed resumes across her desk to Alex. "The other six, they're just," she paused and then sighed, "not even worth reading."

Alex looked up. His eyes widened. Alex was a manager who needed to fill a vacant position in his team, and quickly. "Who's this guy? Why can't we get him?" asked Alex enthusiastically.

"Nick Chisholm. He's worked for a couple of the majors, and he's got great experience. I just know he'd also be talking with other majors who pay better, have a better culture, and better career options," answered Sarah.

"Can you get me a coffee meeting with him? We've had such a bad run with people resigning lately. We just need someone great to come in and turn the team around," Alex replied.

"Will do," Sarah said. "It doesn't hurt to have a go."

Alex had given Sarah the nickname "Sarah HRH." It was short for "Human Resources from Heaven," a nod to her English heritage and a play on the queen's title of Her Royal Highness, for Alex believed that she was, in fact, true royalty. Sarah had supported Alex through many sticky HR situations when he either needed to hire quickly or had a problem employee with whom he needed help. And once again, Sarah HRH had delivered and set up the meeting between Alex and Nick at a downtown coffee shop. This was perfect for Alex because he knew once he could spend time in a casual setting with a candidate, he had a great chance of converting them, of getting them to sign a contract and join the team.

As Alex and Nick met, worked through the pleasantries, and started talking about the opportunity for Nick to come and work with Alex instead of one of the majors, Alex could feel he was beginning to win, little by little. He loved watching the company story, the pay and conditions, the team, and the work begin to sway Nick. By the end of the meeting, Alex felt just a little confident that Nick would join. As Alex left the coffee shop, he couldn't help but smile just a little. Getting someone with Nick Chisholm's experience to sign up could finally turn his team around. Alex reflected on the perfect timing as he returned to the office. For having Nick sign up in the next two weeks would allow Alex to take his planned holiday to Hawaii before Nick started, and he could enjoy a real break, knowing that his hiring problem was solved.

It didn't go exactly to plan. Nick got two other offers, as Alex later learned, including one in Newtown that he almost took. But Alex was determined to get the deal, and because he'd built the relationship with Nick at the coffee shop and kept in close contact, he knew how Nick's situation was developing. So when Nick received an offer at a higher rate, Alex was able to get the higher salary approved by his manager and have Nick sign the contract and join the team.

"We might start calling you the candidate whisperer!" joked Sarah as Alex passed her the employment contract.

"I couldn't do it without HRH!" laughed Alex. "But seriously, we've been really behind in my department. How can we get Nick up to speed as quickly as possible?"

"He's got a lot of experience," replied Sarah. "I'm sure he will be a good fit."

Alex nodded in acceptance of Sarah's reasoning and left her office, thinking that with only two days until his Hawaii holiday, everything was in order.

•

"Look at you with your Hawaii tan!" remarked Sarah two weeks later as they walked into the meeting room to welcome Alex for his first day.

"It was just what the doctor ordered. I'm all better!" laughed Alex. "It was so good to get a break. We're all set for Nick, right? The laptop and everything?" Alex asked.

"All ready to go," replied Sarah with a smile.

In the following days, Alex showed Nick around, and things seemed to get even better. Nick's experience was a breath of fresh air for Alex, and at one point, Alex even encouraged Nick to "Have a play around with the software" because Alex knew that someone with Nick's experience would find it easy to figure out.

It was great to have a new team member with experience that Alex could trust. "The tide has turned," Alex thought to himself. "Finally, our problems are behind us, and we're starting to build a great team."

At a meeting six months later, Nick updated the team on a project his team was running. "He's coming along well," Alex thought, smiling to himself. "He's turning into a productive, useful, and valuable team member."

After the meeting, Alex walked toward Nick to let him know how pleased he was with his progress. But when Nick noticed Alex approaching, his expression quickly changed. It was as though Nick had seen a ghost. Before Alex could speak, Nick said, "Hey Alex, have you got a minute?"

● ● ●

There's a moment when a person signs an employment contract that several of your worries lift from your shoulders.

"I've solved that problem," you may think, "I've got a person in that role. Let's see how they work out."

But that's not what the new hire is thinking.

They probably think, "I've solved that problem. I've secured that role. Let's see how this new employer works out."

According to a survey by the Aberdeen Group, 87 percent of new employees aren't fully committed to a new job for the first six months. A further study by BambooHR revealed that the average company loses one in six new hires each month for the first three months.

Just because you've hired someone into a role, there is no evidence that they are committed to you or will stay. The onus is now on you as their manager to increase their engagement, their connection to the team and the firm, and to activate their pride. Remember, they were probably speaking with other potential employers only a few weeks ago.

Let's consider the onboarding period from two perspectives: the manager's point of view and the new hire's point of view.

	Manager's point of view	New hire's point of view
Employment contract signed	Is all the paperwork in order? How can we get this new hire up to speed as quickly as possible?	Is this the right job for me? Is this the right company for me? Is the contract as expected?
Two weeks before the start day	Is everything organised for the new hire's first day? Computer, paperwork, meetings with HR booked? How can we get this new hire up to speed as quickly as possible? Does the new hire know about the workplace rules and regulations?	What will it be like to work with my new manager? What will my new job involve? What are my co-workers like? I wonder what will happen on my first day?
Start day	Does the new hire have all the right resources to do their job? Are we making a good impression?	Will I get a warm welcome? Maybe I will meet a friend or get a welcome pack? Perhaps even a morning tea to welcome me?
First week	Is the paperwork complete? Is everyone following the onboarding process?	Does my manager care about me? Do I know who to talk to if there's an issue? Have I made the right decision?
First month	Is the new hire settling in? Are there any issues that need resolving?	Am I actively contributing to the business? Do I understand what is expected of me? Do I know where to go with any unresolved issues?
Second month	Is the new hire productive and contributing to the organisation?	How can I do better in my job? How can I make this role mine? Do I have a best friend at work?
Third month	Is the new hire a productive, useful, and valuable member of the team?	Do I love my job? Can I keep learning and growing in this company? Can I see myself here in two years? Can I do my best work here?

Figure 1.1 **Manager's view compared to the new hire's view**

When a new hire signs a contract and the recruiting phase has concluded, your firm enters a trial period with them in their mind for up to six months. If your recruiting process has worked well and produced a potential fit, you must understand that the new hire needs to successfully fit from both your perspective and their perspective throughout their onboarding.

Failing to activate a person's pride for the organization, product, manager, and team and failing to help them understand how to succeed in their role leads to unhappiness and attrition.

Once a person signs an employment contract, one of the manager's essential tasks is activating and amplifying that person's pride. We can achieve this through several touchpoints in the onboarding process.

CHAPTER 2

The Employee Weapon
of Mass Destruction

Alex was rattled. His heart was thumping.

This wasn't his first rodeo. He knew the tell-tale signs of a team member who was about to resign. Alex had seen the anxiety on their face, and the dreaded question "Have you got a minute?" had sadly become a joke between him and Sarah.

But not this time. This just didn't make sense. Nick was such a good fit. He had only been there six months and was progressing so well. Only a few minutes ago, during Nick's presentation, Alex marvelled at how well Nick was developing. "Nick wasn't resigning," Alex thought, "it must be something else."

The team loved Nick, and he loved them. Surely not Nick. In fact, definitely not Nick.

And with that quick recovery, Alex turned to Nick and said, "Sure, Nick, let's head back to my office." Alex made light chat about the other team members' presentations at the meeting they'd just attended as the two strolled. This short chat calmed Alex even further. "What was I worried about?" Alex wondered.

Alex confidently walked into his office, not knowing what Nick was about to talk about, yet relieved it wasn't going to be about resignation.

Nick followed him into the office and closed the door. Before Alex even had a chance to ask, "So what's up, Nick?" Nick stated, "I've had an offer that's too good to refuse."

"Oh," came Alex's reply. He tried to maintain his composure, despite feeling as though someone had just sat on his chest.

"Yeah, it's been good here, but I've just got to do the right thing by my family," said Nick as he reached into the breast pocket of his jacket and pulled out what Alex and Sarah referred to as the Employee Weapon of Mass Destruction, a typed and signed resignation letter.

"You've been doing so well," said Alex, thinking fast but trying to look calm. "If they're offering more money, I could head upstairs to get more money for you with what you've already achieved. Just so we can keep you. I'm sure they'd be up for that."

"Thanks, Alex," said Nick. He paused just long enough for Alex to gain a glimmer of hope. "But I've already decided. Plus, I've signed a contract."

"You've signed a contract with us!" thought Alex. But he remained professional and said what he was supposed to. "Okay, not much I can do then," said Alex. "I guess we've got two weeks to go."

"Thanks for your support, Alex. It's been great working here." And with that, Nick stood, turned, and walked out of the office, leaving the signed resignation letter on Alex's desk. Alex looked back at the empty seat that Nick sat in only moments before, and he thought about his team before Nick, the years of mistakes, poor productivity, and a series of resignations. Nick was supposed to be the end of it, the beginning of this team's turnaround.

As Alex walked into Sarah's office, she could immediately tell by the look on his face that he'd just received a resignation. She'd seen it too many times before. "Who?" she asked as Alex walked in and closed the door. "Not Ramesh, surely not Olivia?"

Alex stopped before he sat down. "Nick," he said, dropping Nick's resignation letter onto Sarah's desk.

"Oh no, Alex."

The two of them discussed just how bad it was of Nick to leave after only six months, why it's so hard to find good people nowadays, and why Nick's generation is so self-centred.

Then Alex looked at his phone and said, "Is that the time? I'm going out tonight to a barbeque with some friends. I guess we'd better put an advert out there for Nick's replacement."

"Will do," replied Sarah. "Never mind, we'll get it right this time."

•

Alex hadn't met Isabelle before. She'd been dating his friend Ben for about two months, and Ben was keen to have everyone meet her at the barbeque he was hosting. For many years Ben had been a bachelor, and for the last two months, Alex hadn't heard much from Ben. He'd been even quieter about Isabelle. After the devastating news from Nick earlier that day, Alex didn't feel like going out but knew how important it was to Ben.

"Good to meet you, Alex. Ben talks about you all the time. How was your day?" asked Isabelle as the pair shook hands by the warmth of Ben's barbeque.

Alex couldn't help but sigh. He knew he shouldn't bring his work problems to this chat, but it was all he could think about. "Pretty crappy, actually. A guy on my team quit. He was just perfect, and then today, out of nowhere, he handed in his resignation after only six months."

Isabelle looked confused, and Alex knew he shouldn't have discussed work problems; after all, it was the first time they'd met.

"What happened during his onboarding?" Isabelle asked.

"What a strange question," Alex thought. Still, he was comforted that she was okay to talk about work. "Usual stuff. He completed the paperwork, got his computer, and we got him working."

"No, that's the induction," said Isabelle, "like a license to operate that inducts him into the firm and enables him to work. I'm talking about his onboarding."

"Oh. He was really experienced, we showed him our systems, and he was good to go," came Alex's reply. "He was a good fit, but he got offered more money in the end."

Isabelle paused maybe a little longer than she should have before she replied, "Well, where I work, we've got a very specific definition of onboarding. We take someone from outside our organization and make them a productive, independent, and confident team member who understands the culture, the technical and process expectations, and your expectations as their manager. Then if we're confident at the end of the onboarding, we change their status from 'new hire' to 'successful fit,' which means that the new hire fully understands how to succeed. It means that we've caused them to successfully fit into the firm."

"Sounds like a lot of work. How long does that take?" replied Alex.

"Ninety days because that's when their legal probation ends," said Isabelle. "If they're not going to be a successful fit, we can exit them before then. But what really works is that we build a role scorecard to understand what success means in the role, and then every new hire has a weekly meeting with their manager during the first ninety days."

Alex was a little surprised. "That sounds like a lot of work. Anyway, I've got a great HR lady, Sarah, who takes care of all that stuff," he replied.

"Yeah, we found it works best when our managers run the onboarding," Isabelle said.

Alex was bemused. "We just don't have time for all that. We've been so busy fixing problems and trying to hire people. We're just not a big business with those kinds of resources," said Alex. Before Isabelle could explain that she worked for a firm with a staff of only fifty, Ben interrupted, yelling, "Come and get it!" Dinner was served.

Alex didn't get to chat any further with Isabelle that night, but she seemed a great match for Ben. When he arrived home, Alex grabbed his phone to check what meetings he had the following day. As he scrolled through the meetings in his calendar, he remembered with a jolt his 2 pm monthly meeting the next day with his boss Dave, where he would have to explain Nick's resignation.

• • •

Why do employees leave a company?

In the previous chapter, when learning of Nick's resignation, we saw Alex's first response was to offer more money. This might be a typical manager's reaction.

According to Leigh Branham, 89 percent of managers say people leave because they want more money. Yet when he analysed over twenty thousand exit interviews with employees about why they really leave a company, 88 percent of employees said it wasn't the money, but other reasons, as shown in Figure 2.1 from Leigh's book, *The 7 Hidden Reasons Employees Leave: How to Recognize the Subtle Signs and Act Before It's Too Late.*

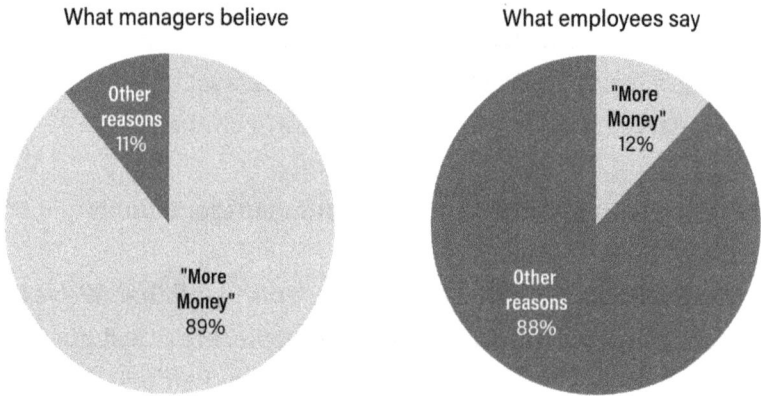

What managers believe   **What employees say**

Other reasons 11%

"More Money" 89%

"More Money" 12%

Other reasons 88%

Figure 2.1 **What managers believe about why employees leave vs. why employees actually leave**

In the book, Branham identified the seven hidden reasons people leave:

1 *The job or workplace was not as expected*

2 *The mismatch between job and person*

3 *Too little coaching and feedback*

4 *Too few growth and advancement opportunities*

5 *Feeling devalued and unrecognized*

6 *Stress from overwork and work-life balance*

7 *Loss of trust and confidence in senior leaders*

An effective ninety-day onboarding process can significantly impact or overcome almost every one of these factors. We will discuss this approach in the coming chapters.

In a separate survey, 90 percent of respondents said that the retention of new hires is an issue in their organization. Nearly all (98 percent) said that onboarding programs are key to retention efforts.

●

When Isabelle and Alex were chatting, Isabelle explained that Alex didn't take Nick through an onboarding but only what she described as an induction, as it was focused on completing paperwork and getting him a computer.

Let's define some of the processes adjacent to onboarding.

Induction is where you admit a new employee to an organization or role. It's like a license to operate; it provides the employee the ability to participate in the organization. You might classify a new hire as having been inducted when they have completed the forms to get paid and pay taxes, know their computer login and how to access their email, and have been issued security access cards.

Orientation is the process of helping a person become familiar with a location or situation. It is how they come to know their way around. After a new hire has completed orientation, they should know the location of the IT and HR departments and who to talk with if they need help. They should also know emergency procedures and the locations of the exits and restrooms. Orientation might also include things like car parking arrangements or an explanation of the org chart and who does what.

Training is where you teach an employee a new skill or behaviour or help them to improve an existing one. Training applies both to existing employees and new hires during the onboarding process.

Once trained on a subject, new hires within the onboarding process should understand the processes and systems required to do their job. Or, to put it another way, they should understand "the way we do things here."

Onboarding is the process of taking someone from outside your organization and making them a productive, independent, and confident member of your team who understands the culture, the technical and process expectations, and your expectations as their manager.

Understanding why employees leave and how to define processes related to onboarding is important. Also important to note is the significance of why an onboarding process should be ninety-days.

In the late nineteenth century, German psychologist Hermann Ebbinghaus tested his memory over a series of studies to understand how people remember information and how the mind loses information over time. The graph he plotted is represented in Figure 2.2, demonstrating how information disappears exponentially once we learn something.

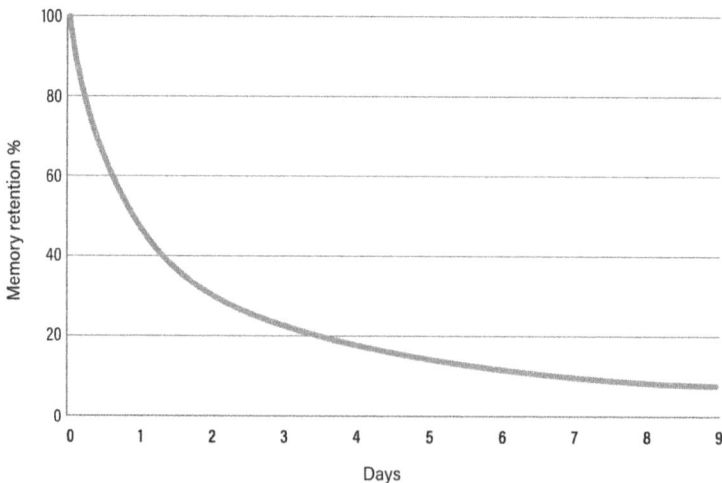

Figure 2.2 **The Forgetting Curve**

One day after learning new information, our retention drops to around 55 percent. However, by the time a week has passed, retention plummets to about 10 percent. This incredible discovery is known as Ebbinghaus's Forgetting Curve and is one of the reasons most onboarding processes are ineffective.

In my research for this book, I surveyed over 1,100 CEOs and hiring managers globally across various organizations, from less than ten employees to over five hundred employees. I asked many questions, including the duration of their onboarding process and how well new hires understood the managers' expectations, the culture, and the processes after their onboarding.

As you can see in Figure 2.3, when an onboarding process lasts for a week or less, about 34 percent of respondents agree that once complete, their onboarding process leads to recent hires understanding the manager's expectations, the culture, and the company processes.

Yet if the onboarding process takes ninety days, about 53 percent of respondents agree with the same questions.

This difference of around 19 percent is just one example of onboarding debt—an absence of understanding in the recent hire.

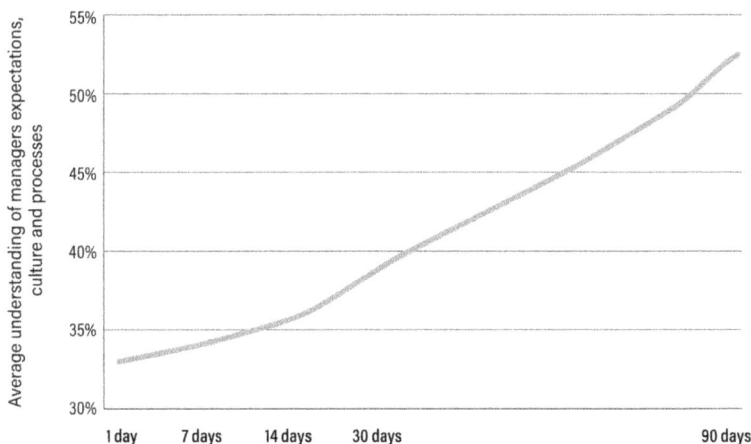

Figure 2.3 Longer onboarding leads to a better understanding of expectations and processes

Human nature often leads managers to provide the minimum onboarding time, teaching essential items only once. Human biology means that new hires will likely forget 90 percent of what they are taught within a week, as shown in Figure 2.2.

However, not all is lost. Subsequent research found that when we re-teach a concept, people remember it once again. For example, the first time information is re-taught, people once again forget 90 percent of what they learned within a week. But that forgetting will differ from the initial forgetting rate, as shown in Figure 2.4. When that information is taught a third time, something remarkable happens in the brain. Instead of forgetting 90 percent, a person forgets only 50 percent. Finally, when taught a fourth time, a person will retain 90 percent of the information!

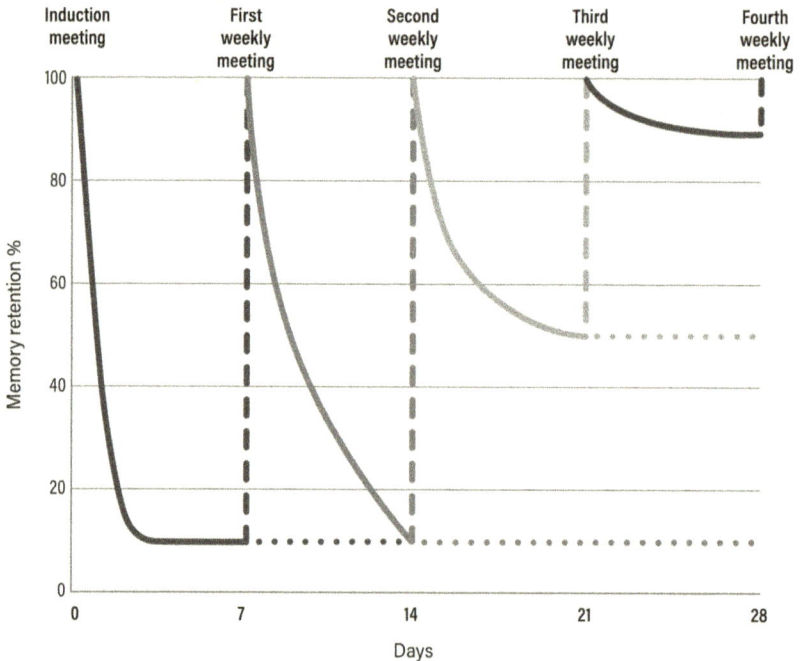

Figure 2.4 Overcoming the Forgetting Curve

Managers need to overcome the Forgetting Curve during this stage and be confident that new hires can understand what they've been taught. However, this doesn't mean repeating the same information for four weeks in a row. For example, you could tell a different story about each of your core values each week. In this way, you reinforce the same core values from different perspectives.

CHAPTER 3

What Are You Doing To Them?

"Not again. Tell me you're joking," said Dave as he looked down, putting his forehead in one hand. Dave was an old-school entrepreneur with one hundred things going through his mind all the time, twenty new projects on his list (which he rarely completed), and one method of communicating: directly!

"I'm afraid not," replied Alex, hoping that was as bad as the reprimand would get.

Of course, it immediately got much worse when Dave replied with words that would hit him like a baseball bat.

"What are you doing to them?" asked Dave. Suddenly the thoughts Alex prepared about the hiring market and how young people today weren't committed melted away. Alex's boss was blaming him for the people who were leaving. As he reeled at the idea, he replied with what might have been the worst possible answer.

"I don't know," he said, almost trying to catch the words before they left his lips, knowing that would be ammunition for Dave's reply.

"Well, if you don't know what you're doing to them that's making them leave, what are we paying you for?"

Alex knew enough to stay quiet, for when Dave got upset, he started giving instructions to fix the problem. "Can you start advertising for the replacement? And two things. I want you to come to our next monthly meeting with how much this is costing us and your plan on how you're going to fix this problem."

•

"So this is what writer's block feels like," thought Alex. He'd been looking at a blank page on his laptop for almost thirty minutes, trying to think about how to measure the cost and build a plan. Alex knew he could lose his job if Dave wasn't impressed with his calculations and plan. It seemed straightforward: just list how many people left his department and how much each one cost. But Alex knew that Dave wouldn't accept that. Alex could almost see Dave saying, "And what else?" That wasn't enough and wouldn't end well. Alex's calculations and plan needed to be better than that if he was going to have a future at the firm.

He then thought about his chat with Isabelle a few days earlier and why she first asked after learning about Nick's resignation: "What happened during his onboarding?" From how she described onboarding at her company, Alex was certain that she must work for a big firm, but she was really clear about their onboarding and what happened at the end. Alex recalled the eight words she used: "The new hire fully understands how to succeed." His talk with Isabelle was brief, but it felt like he was assembling a jigsaw puzzle. Finally, all these pieces looked like they might fit together.

Alex replayed in his mind what he could recall from the conversation with Isabelle, trying to develop a central idea for his plan. "If new hires don't understand the culture, the technical and process expectations, and your expectations as their manager, there will be a price to pay. This leads to a dysfunctional culture, more mistakes and rework, and frustrated leadership, because new hires don't know their expectations. But it's also frustrating for new hires, and they might leave."

As Alex looked over and over at the words he'd written, he thought about just how many people had left his team, how frustrated he was at the constant problems and rework, how often he was perplexed at people not doing things the right way, and finally, how crappy the culture was. Alex thought this must be costing his team alone hundreds of thousands of dollars. Dave was going to be even angrier at the next monthly meeting. But if Alex had a good plan, Dave would buy it. Alex needed to call Ben, get Isabelle's number, and learn more about Isabelle's hiring and onboarding, and fast.

"We broke up," said Ben when Alex called, sounding almost relieved. "I'm a bachelor again, baby!"

"No, but Ben, I really need to talk with her; my job depends on it," said Alex.

Ben paused. "Oh, yeah, I can't give you her number. We had this big messy fight, and she's angry. She doesn't want to hear anything about me ever again."

Alex sighed. He needed to figure this out himself. He looked back to his computer and thought again about what Isabelle had said: "The new hire fully understands how to succeed." Nick should have understood how to succeed because he'd worked for the majors and had years of experience. But there was more to it than just that. One of the things Alex liked about his job was that they did things differently than the majors. The processes weren't so stuffy and rigid, and the culture was more entrepreneurial and maybe a little more fun. In fact, it was so different that it would probably be pretty tough to grow up at the majors and move here.

And then, just like getting slapped in the face with a wet fish, Alex realized that Nick didn't understand how to succeed at his firm. And even worse, it was because Alex didn't help Nick to understand.

Maybe Dave, at his most brutal, was right. Maybe when Dave said, "What are you doing to them?" the question should have been, "What aren't you doing to them?"

Looking back to his computer and the plan he was building, Alex thought about Nick going about his day trying to navigate their processes and software compared to the places he'd previously worked. He thought about coming from the bureaucratic culture at the majors to the informal, entrepreneurial culture here. Then he thought about Nick's old boss and how different he would be to work for.

"There's a real cost here," Alex said to Sarah over the phone, keen to share his newfound insight. "Because Nick didn't really understand how to succeed, that meant he didn't know how we do things, leading to more errors, issues, rework, and lower productivity. It's as though his lack of understanding was a liability on the company balance sheet. He might not have completely understood, but his understanding could have been much better."

"Well, how would you rate his understanding of how to succeed out of ten?" enquired Sarah.

"Phew." He paused. "Across the three areas of cultural, technical, and process and my expectations, I'd say a six out of ten."

Sarah thought for a moment before replying. "So you're saying that Nick, one of our best hires, didn't understand 40 percent of how to succeed in his role here, and that is a liability the company carries, which causes errors and lower productivity?"

"Yeah," replied Alex.

"So that liability, that debt, is in everyone who works here?" Sarah responded.

"I guess so," Alex replied.

Sarah continued, "That must be enormous across everyone. I mean, the cost of errors, having to do things again, just the cost of productivity alone!"

"I hadn't thought about the whole team," said Alex. "You're right. It looks like my plan for Dave is coming together."

Sarah was quick to respond. "You forgot one thing. You've found the cost of misunderstanding. That's the intangible cost. But there's still the financial cost, things like attrition and rehiring. That's where the hard dollar costs will surface."

"Oh," Alex replied. "On top of this, I don't know how Dave will take that."

• • •

How do companies inadvertently create bad cultures?

Many of today's thinkers and writers discuss identifying a bad culture and what to do about it. But few, if any, ask how bad cultures occur. It's like there's a disease, and all the experts are talking about how to identify if you have the disease and what to do if you have it, but no one asks how one catches it in the first place.

If a good culture is the foundation of success, then understanding the cause of bad cultures, not just the symptoms, is one of the most important things that a leader who seeks success must do.

Imagine you assembled a group of ten random people into a team. However, you provided no instruction, guidance, or training about the culture, technical and process expectations, and leader's expectations. What would be the resulting culture of the team in a few months or a few years? At best, it would be a roll of the dice.

Maybe you could get lucky, and it would be okay.

But more than likely, people would do what they think is right. They would try to do the right thing. But every one of the ten people's interpretations of the right thing, in any situation, could be different.

Those different perspectives can lead to misunderstandings and differences of opinion, and over time, those minor issues can compound and create a dysfunctional culture.

Now consider the opposite—a team of ten random people you provide with a detailed onboarding plan. Over ninety days, you help them understand, learn, apply, and then embed the cultural, technical, and process expectations and the leader's expectations to be a successful fit.

Equally, those who are an unsuccessful fit depart after that ninety-day onboarding.

The result is that the team who participated in the onboarding will understand what is right. There will be fewer misunderstandings and differences of opinion. There will be better communication about what the team agrees on and a much lower chance of a dysfunctional culture.

The higher the onboarding debt, the more likely an organization will have cultural issues.

Think about the length of your onboarding process, and then consider that 49 percent of respondents I surveyed had a seven-day or less onboarding process, and 83 percent had fourteen days or less of onboarding. The vast majority of onboarding processes are one or two weeks. That's five or ten working days to maximize understanding and minimize onboarding debt.

There is a direct connection between the onboarding process and the culture within an organization.

In my research, 85 percent of respondents with a ninety-day onboarding process agreed or somewhat agreed with the statement that *our onboarding process positively contributes to our culture*. Yet, as shown in Figure 3.1, that drops to 50 percent for those with a one-day onboarding process.

People with a longer onboarding process are more likely to agree that it positively contributes to their culture.

Our onboarding process positively contributes to our culture

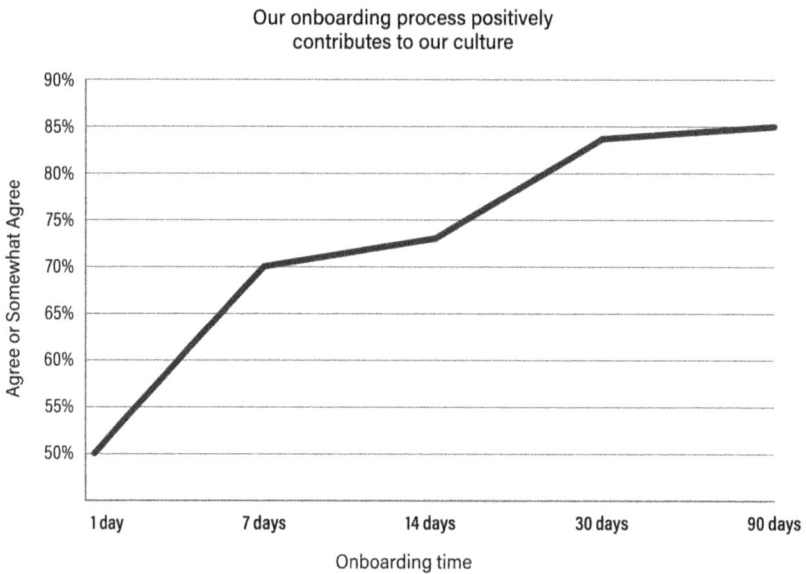

Figure 3.1 **Longer onboarding positively impacts culture**

In addition to asking respondents about their understanding of culture, I asked them about their understanding of managers' expectations and company processes.

As illustrated in Figure 3.2, the length of an onboarding process impacts a new hire's understanding across these three areas by an approximate 14 percent increase from the thirty-day to ninety-day processes. This is in keeping with much of my research findings: the most significant impacts occur after thirty-day onboarding periods.

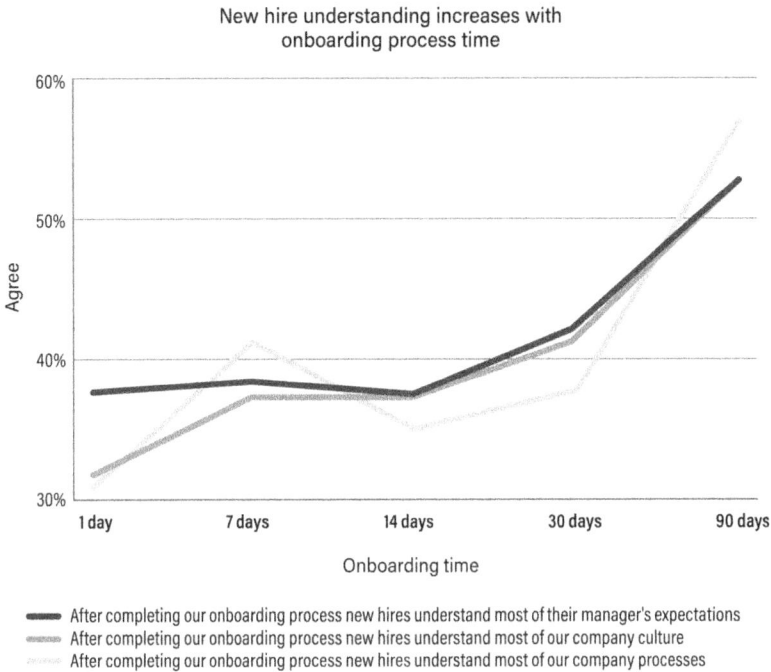

Figure 3.2 **Impact of onboarding process time on new hire understanding**

When a single hire is onboarded poorly, onboarding debt accrues. This is significant in terms of the potential productivity we miss out on for that individual. But teams are complex, and we must also factor in the debt generated for all team members because of that new hire, how they interact, and any existing onboarding debt that other team members may carry.

If there are two people in a team, there are only two points of communication – my interaction with you and your interaction with me. If there are three people, there are six points. Add just one more person and take that number to four people in a team, and there are twelve points of communication, as shown in Figure 3.3.

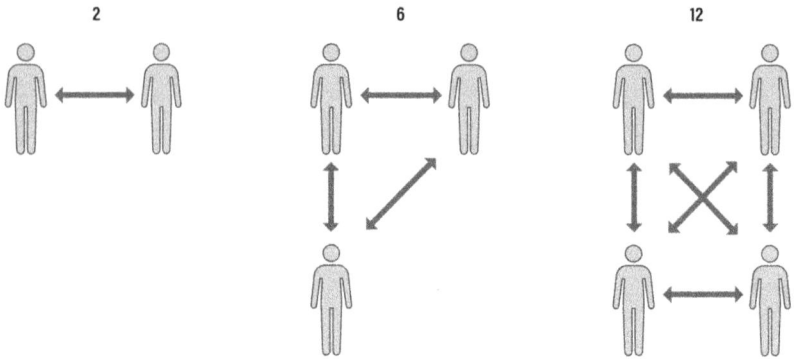

Figure 3.3 **Points of communication for different team sizes**

This increasing complexity makes the onboarding debt ever more expensive to service. For example, suppose you have a team with each person carrying an onboarding debt of 37 percent. This complexity across different communication channels grows exponentially, and the debt is incurred much faster than the team's growth.

If we refer to Figure 3.4, we can see how individual onboarding debt impacts team onboarding debt. With a team of two, if person A understands 80 percent of the culture, their manager's expectations, and technical and process expectations, and person B understands 50 percent, then the team's average understanding is 80 + 50 / 2 = 65 percent. Therefore, they have a team onboarding debt of 35 percent. But this is only multiplied through two points of communication.

With a team of three, if person A has a 35 percent understanding, person B has 60 percent, and person C has 85 percent, then the average team understanding is 60 percent, and the onboarding debt is 40 percent. Remember, misunderstanding can occur anywhere within six communication points in a team of three. The presence of a top performer in this team doesn't override the risk of issues arising from misunderstanding.

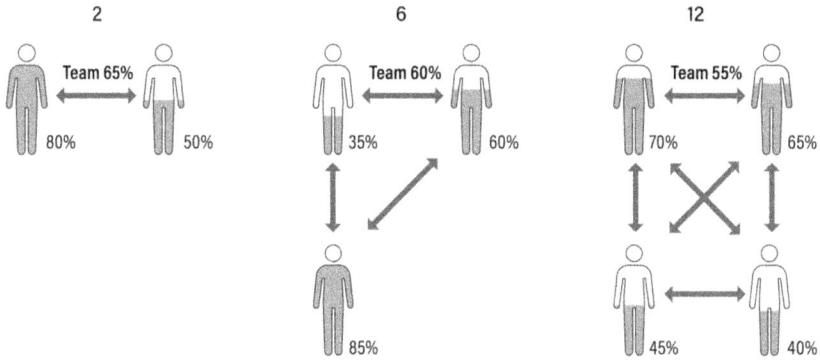

Figure 3.4 **Team onboarding debt as a team grows**

As we grow our teams, the individual onboarding debt remains. People find workarounds, learn lessons, and figure things out, so the individual debt brought into a team will fade beyond their initial ninety days, but people's bad habits will become entrenched.

CHAPTER 4

How Much Has It Cost Us?

"It looks like a pin-up board from a murder investigation on a TV show!" said Sarah when she walked into Alex's office. "The only thing missing is the bits of string between the pins that prove you're beginning to lose it!"

"Huh," replied Alex with half a laugh. "Grab a seat, and let me explain."

Alex pointed to the left of the board. "We've already touched on the cost of misunderstanding and how it's cost us through rework and errors. That's next. First, let's start with the cost of hiring. I found an online guide that helps to explain it. You can see it here." Alex pointed to his pinboard at the chart shown in Figure 4.1.

Role	Cost of a hire
Entry-level / junior roles	50% of annual salary
Mid-level individual contributors	100% of annual salary
Mid-level managers	100% of annual salary
Senior-level individual contributors	125% of annual salary
Senior-level managers	125% of annual salary
Executives	200% of annual salary

Figure 4.1 The cost of hiring

"Hmm, I like it, but some of those numbers seem a little high," responded Sarah.

"That's exactly what I thought!" said Alex. "But when I looked deeper, I noticed that it's not only the cost inside HR for things like recruiters' costs, advertising, and HR time. There's also the cost outside HR. That's things like handing over the work, covering workload with reduced productivity, severance cost, and interviewing time."

"Yeah, I guess," Sarah replied. "That's why managers always hate it when someone leaves. There's a huge workload for them to close and rehire."

"You got it!" said Alex. "Now look at how much that's cost us here at ACME manufacturing in the past year. I've added each role we've needed to rehire for and the salary."

Alex pointed to another chart on his pin board, as shown in Figure 4.2.

Role	Number of hires in the past year (a)	Average salary (b)	Hire cost (c)	Total cost = a x b x c
Entry level / junior roles	7	$35,000	50% of annual salary	$122,500
Mid-level individual contributors	3	$65,000	100% of annual salary	$195,000
Mid-level managers	2	$70,000	100% of annual salary	$140,000
Senior-level individual contributors	1	$90,000	125% of annual salary	$112,500
Senior-level managers	2	$100,000	125% of annual salary	$250,000
Executives	1	$150,000	200% of annual salary	$300,000
	17		Total Cost	$1,120,000

Figure 4.2 Total cost of hiring example

Alex went on, "We didn't create any new roles this year. We began the year with one hundred staff members and ended with one hundred staff members. But the seventeen people that resigned who needed to be replaced cost $1,120,000."

Sarah leaned back in her chair, the weight of accumulating costs dawning on her. "But we couldn't have zero attrition. I meant, what if someone retired?" she said.

"Yes! Now look over here." Alex responded, his eyes widening as he pointed to the chart shown in Figure 4.3. "If we could halve it from seventeen to eight, that would be achievable. Then it would take our attrition cost from $1,120,000 to $442,500, saving $677,500."

Role	Number of hires in the past year. (a)	Average salary (b)	Hire cost (c)	Total cost = a x b x c
Entry level / junior roles	4	$35,000	50% of annual salary	$70,000
Mid-level individual contributors	1	$65,000	100% of annual salary	$65,000
Mid-level managers	1	$70,000	100% of annual salary	$70,000
Senior-level individual contributors	1	$90,000	125% of annual salary	$112,500
Senior-level managers	1	$100,000	125% of annual salary	$125,000
Executives	0	$150,000	200% of annual salary	$0
	8		Total Cost	$442,500

Figure 4.3 Example of the impact of reduced attrition on the total cost of hiring

"Oh wow. So what's that?" asked Sarah, pointing to a similar table on the pin board.

"That's productivity. I'm trying to figure out the cost of the misunderstanding we discussed. We know our boss, Dave. He won't accept anything without a dollar figure against it," said Alex, looking at the chart shown in Figure 4.4. "So, we've hired seventeen new people in the last year at a total annual salary cost of $1,020,000. But we need to make a profit on those salaries."

"Of course," replied Sarah with interest.

Alex continued, "So let's assume we need to make $2 for every $1 we pay in salaries to these seventeen new staff. This would mean the company would expect to make $2.04 million in gross profit from these people. Still with me, HRH?" Alex enquired with a smile.

"Yep, keep going," Sarah responded.

"I suspect that it's currently taking nine months for our new hires to become fully productive because we're doing very little to help them understand how to succeed any earlier. Let's think about a misunderstanding of, say, 40 percent, with a six-out-of-ten rating on their understanding. With the longer time it takes to become fully productive, we're losing another $648,000."

"You've lost me now!" laughed Sarah.

Alex laughed, "I get it. Here's the point. I think I can prove that our ineffective onboarding process is costing us just under $1.1 million per year."

"But, we're only a $30 million company," said Sarah. "If your calculations are correct, Dave's gonna love you, and I'm going to get more HR resources!"

"Let's take one step at a time," replied Alex as he stood to walk out of his office.

Role	Number of hires in the past year (a)	Average salary (b)	Average productivity = b x $2 LER (c)	Lost productivity cost = c x 0.4 x 0.75 (d)	Total cost = a x d
Entry level / junior roles	7	$35,000	$70,000	$21,000	$147,000
Mid-level individual contributors	3	$65,000	$130,000	$39,000	$117,000
Mid-level managers	2	$70,000	$140,000	$42,000	$84,000
Senior-level individual contributors	1	$90,000	$180,000	$54,000	$54,500
Senior-level managers	2	$100,000	$200,000	$60,000	$120,000
Executives	1	$150,000	$300,000	$90,000	$90,000
	17			Total Cost	$648,000

Figure 4.4 Productivity cost example for new hires in the first year

Later that day, Alex turned a corner in the office and almost collided with Dave.

"Woah, Alex, what's the rush?" Dave asked, and before Alex could reply, Dave added, "Anyone else quit on you?"

As much as he wanted to respond with a clever answer, Alex knew there was only one way to reply: laugh and move on. "No, thankfully. But the costs and plan are coming together well for our monthly meeting."

"How much has it cost us?" asked Dave, never one to hold back. Alex knew this was all moving faster than it should, but he had to give an answer to prove that he was progressing. Plus, he was a little excited about the findings.

"It's looking just over $1 million per year," Alex responded.

Dave snapped back, seeming sceptical. "You got calculations to prove that?"

"They're not finished yet," said Alex, "but they're close and will be done by our meeting."

What Dave said next took Alex by surprise. "I knew you had it in you," said Dave, smiling. Alex wasn't used to compliments from Dave, and he smiled in response, taking a moment to enjoy it.

But the positive feeling from Dave's comment wasn't to last. Dave started walking away, then stopped, turned back, and said, "Oh, how's the new guy Ed going? It's been a few months now."

Alex's mind started racing. In his excitement about the costs and plan for Dave, he'd forgotten all about his new hire Ed. As Alex thought about Ed and looked across the office workstations, one thing immediately came to his mind. Four. Alex instinctively rated Ed's understanding of how to succeed at a four out of ten.

"Good," is all Alex could say as he attempted an unconvincing smile. But, at that moment, Alex realized that Ed would never succeed at ACME manufacturing. And Ed's problem had just become Alex's problem.

• • •

As Alex has shown us through the examples in this chapter, you must consider three aspects when weighing how much an ineffective onboarding process might cost you.

Firstly, the cost per hire. Without a business analyst on hand to consider the many complex scenarios related to the cost of hiring, you can use the simple table shown by Alex in Figure 4.1, which should give you an off-the-shelf ballpark estimate of the total hiring cost. If you're looking for a more accurate number, search online for the well-known Bliss-Gately spreadsheet.

When hiring an employee, you probably think about the cost of a job board advert or a recruiter's cost and maybe the time for people in Human Resources to interview a candidate. So perhaps five, ten, or twenty thousand dollars could be considered a reasonable cost to hire.

Why is it then that a manager will groan (and often swear) when someone resigns? Why might a manager keep a new hire that isn't right? These managers experience first-hand the loss of time, effort, and productivity required to get another person into the role, fully understanding the culture, the manager's expectations, and the technical and process expectations. And this cost is entirely outside the HR department.

Therefore, we must consider the cost of hiring in two different areas: firstly, the cost within the HR department, and then the much higher cost outside the HR department, as shown in Figure 4.5.

Event	HR Department cost	Outside HR department cost
Employee departs	Exit interview	Meeting with manager
		Handover of work to a manager, understanding status of work in detail
		Final pay processing in admin
		Team covering the exited team member's workload, reducing their own productivity, or requiring overtime
		Reduced revenue if exited team member is in a sales role
		Severance cost
Hiring	Advertising costs	
	Recruiter costs	
	Interview time	Interview time with potential manager
	Offer negotiation	
Employee starts	Administration	On the job training
		Manager guiding and supervising
		Co-workers answering questions, lowering their productivity
		New hire's productivity takes 1-9 months to reach their predecessor
		Cost to maintain quality or rework as new hire learns

Figure 4.5 **The cost of hiring inside and outside HR**

The second aspect to consider is the total cost of hiring for the past year, as shown in Figure 4.2. As Alex did, consider the total number of employees at the beginning of the year and the total number at the end of the year. For simplicity, ACME hasn't changed the total number of employees in the past year. But maybe your organization has. If that's the case, split out the growth in new roles.

For example, if you started the year with one hundred people and now have 110 people due to growth, then split out the extra ten and focus on the original hundred roles. How many of those initial hundred people are still here? How many rehires did you make in those original hundred roles? This will give you a rough calculation of your attrition rate. For context, the average annual turnover rate for Australia and New Zealand was 17 percent in 2019.

Once you know the number of hires in the past year, you can calculate the cost, as Alex did in Figure 4.2, multiplying the salary by the cost to hire. If you're curious, you can also create different cost-saving scenarios if you reduce your attrition, as Alex did in Figure 4.3.

The third aspect to consider is the productivity cost. Alex used the Labor Efficiency Ratio, or LER, from Greg Crabtree.

This metric for productivity comes from Greg's book *Simple Numbers, Straight Talk, Big Profits!: 4 Keys to Unlock Your Business Potential*. Put simply, this metric tells us how many dollars of gross profit we make for every dollar we pay to employees.

Across a firm, some people within the sales team might produce an LER as high as $6 or $8, whereas a pure administration person might not "produce" any gross profit directly and have an LER of $0. Yet across the entire firm, ACME has an LER of $2, meaning that for every dollar paid in wages, the firm achieves $2 in gross profit.

In the example Alex provided in Figure 4.4, we assume that ACME has a "below-average" onboarding process, creating a 40 percent cost via poor productivity in the first nine months. This lost productivity is calculated using 75 percent of their annual productivity (nine months) multiplied by 0.4 (the productivity cost of 40 percent above).

The cost of an ineffective onboarding process adds up to significant amounts very quickly, as shown. Every firm pays a tangible cost for the quality of their onboarding process, and the costs compound. You might understand how to hire the right people in the right seats, but without an effective onboarding process, you might not understand just how to have those people do the right things in the right way.

CHAPTER 5

A Bad Fit

"Let me check on Ed," said Sarah as she navigated her computer. She clicked around for a moment as Alex waited. "He's got just over one week to go," she concluded.

"So after that, he's in a different category of employment?" Alex asked.

"Something like that," replied Sarah. "After that, he's out of his probation period and becomes a full-time employee with all the standard entitlements. Basically, we can't fire him without fair cause. If he's not going to work out, we've got to take action before the probation is over." Sarah paused, tilted her head, and looked directly at Alex. "He's working out, isn't he?"

"He's." Alex stopped, knowing he was about to create a small mountain of work for himself. "I don't think he's a good fit."

"What?" a shocked Sarah replied. "After Nick's departure, this is going to blow back on you!"

"I know. I keep thinking just how well Ed understands how to succeed, and I keep thinking it's a four out of ten," said Alex.

Sarah stood up, grabbed a marker, and walked across to the whiteboard in her office, recounting her assessment with Alex about Nick. As she erased some old notes, she asked Alex, "How capable is Ed of succeeding?"

"Hmm," Alex replied. "Seven out of ten."

Sarah wrote a seven on the whiteboard. "And you say he is a four in understanding how to succeed?"

Alex nodded as Sarah wrote a four under the seven on the whiteboard. Sarah looked up and out the window, considering other important questions about Ed. "But does he really want to succeed? How would you rate him on that?"

Alex started tapping his chair with his finger as if it helped him think better. "That's the worst part. He wants to succeed. Maybe a seven."

Sarah wrote a seven on the whiteboard and then instinctively tallied the numbers up, writing the number eighteen underneath the others. "Ew," Sarah said, screwing up her face. "Looks like you might have a bad fit. Maybe there's a decision for you to make here."

Alex stared at the whiteboard, not responding. "If I exit Ed, I'll have to rehire and do all the work that comes with that. Yet if I keep Ed, I'm going to burden the organization because he will never be fully productive in the way we need."

As Alex considered his quandary, he suddenly recalled Isabelle describing onboarding at her firm at Ben's barbecue. She'd said, "Then if we're confident at the end of the onboarding, we change their status from 'new hire' to 'successful fit,' which means the new hire fully understands how to succeed. It means we've caused them to successfully fit into the firm."

Alex stood up and walked over to the whiteboard, grabbing a marker. "I didn't cause Ed to successfully fit into the firm, so I can't rate Ed as a successful fit. But also, I can't rate him as an unsuccessful fit for the same reason. It's me. I didn't cause him to fit."

"What?" asked Sarah as she sat down.

Alex continued, "If I keep Ed, I don't know why it worked because I haven't taught him about our expectations and how to succeed here. He just started and got to work. Yet, if I exit Ed, I also don't know why it didn't work for the same reason. I didn't teach him."

Sarah paused and asked, "Is this connected to your 'losing-the-plot' pin-up board?"

Alex tilted his head and said, "Yes. Yes, for sure." He went on to draw a two-by-two matrix, as shown in Figure 5.1, with "new hire stayed" and "new hire left" on the vertical axis, and "onboarding process followed" and "onboarding process not followed" on the horizontal axis. He explained how Isabelle had described onboarding at her firm and why it was so effective for them.

"So, Ed's going to be a bad fit?" enquired Sarah.

"Yep, if I exit him, and worse, I won't really know why it didn't work. We won't learn from it as a company, and we'll be destined to make the same expensive mistakes."

Sarah thought about what Alex was saying and then asked, "What about Nick, our star hire from the majors?"

Alex paused for a moment, gathering his thoughts. "It was my fault. Nick was a good fit," he finally said. "That means we don't know why it worked, so we carried the debt, and it cost us. It wasn't Nick's job to magically understand how to succeed here. It was my job to help him understand."

"What about Ed?" asked Sarah. "We've only got one week to go."

Nick looked drained as he replied, "I don't know."

Alex stood up and turned toward the door when he saw Ed walking toward him, holding a piece of paper. Alex and Sarah turned and looked each other in the eye as Ed knocked on the door and said, "Hey Alex, have you got a minute?"

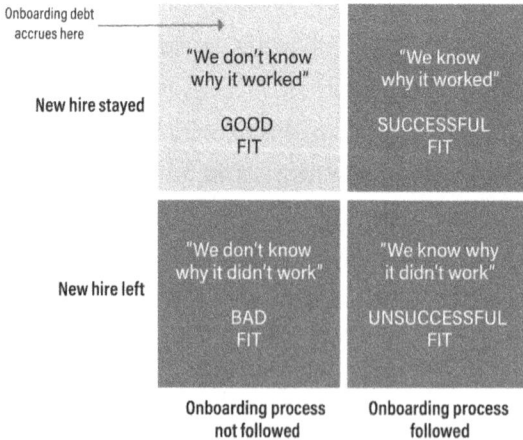

	Onboarding process not followed	Onboarding process followed
New hire stayed *Onboarding debt accrues here* →	"We don't know why it worked" GOOD FIT	"We know why it worked" SUCCESSFUL FIT
New hire left	"We don't know why it didn't work" BAD FIT	"We know why it didn't work" UNSUCCESSFUL FIT

Figure 5.1 Onboarding debt accrual

• • •

Let's consider what happens when a leader reflects on a recent new hire that's gone badly, resulting in that person exiting the company. The leader might explain the exit by saying, "The person was a bad fit."

"How do you know?" one might ask.

"They didn't fit," the leader replies.

"But why?" the other person presses.

"We know they didn't fit because they don't work here anymore!" the leader answers.

The actual reason for the person's departure is never uncovered in this conversation.

Now let's consider another situation where a recently hired person still works at the firm.

"They were a good fit," the leader might explain.

"How do you know?" their co-worker asks.

The leader might then say, "Because they still work here!"

In both cases, the leader will likely consider the individual a good or bad fit *before* they start working for the organization. They do not understand the most important aspect of hiring: when you hire someone, you're provided with a person who is a *potential* fit with your organization. Then the onboarding process takes them from a potential fit to a successful or unsuccessful fit.

To think that a person is a pre-determined good or bad fit is to discount the importance of the onboarding process and its purpose: to make your new hire a productive, independent, and confident member of your team or to confidently validate their exit.

Instead of thinking about people as a good fit or a bad fit, which is a binary mindset that implies their success is entirely out of your control, I recommend using the phrases *successful fit* and *unsuccessful fit*. These phrases indicate that your onboarding process has validated whether the person is a successful fit. This represents a spectrum mindset.

Figure 5.2 illustrates the distinction between the binary mindset and the spectrum mindset. The binary mindset thinks a bad fit definitely won't work and that a good fit definitely will work. On the other hand, with a spectrum mindset, all recent hires are on the spectrum between definitely will work through to definitely won't work. The onboarding process validates whether they are a successful or an unsuccessful fit.

Between contract signing and completing the onboarding process, a person must have the status of *potential fit*. After the onboarding process, their status changes to "successful fit," or they exit with the status of an "unsuccessful fit."

Figure 5.2 **Binary vs. spectrum mindset**

Therefore, as shown in Figure 5.3, the only way a leader can achieve a successful or unsuccessful fit with a spectrum mindset is via the onboarding process.

If you don't know why it worked, how do you know that it did work? Alex believed that Nick worked out well until he resigned six months after joining. But unfortunately, this type of ineffective onboarding is quite common, with Gallup finding that only 12 percent of employees strongly agree their organization does a great job onboarding new employees.

Binary mindset   Spectrum mindset

"good fit"   "bad fit"   "successful fit"   "unsuccessful fit"

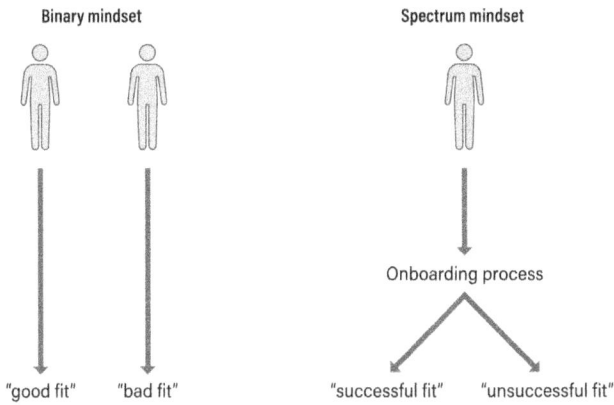

Figure 5.3 **The onboarding process is the only way to determine a successful or unsuccessful fit**

If you have followed a best practice onboarding process and the new hire has stayed, you should be able to say, "We know why it worked." If you have followed a best practice onboarding process and the new hire has left, you should be able to say, "We know why it didn't work."

The day you hire someone, they become a potential fit: there is a potential that they could fit well into the role they've been hired to perform. When you put that person through your onboarding process, you will know whether you are successful or unsuccessful in your attempt to have them fit your role.

CHAPTER 6

Luck Is When Preparation Meets Opportunity

"Refreshing the resume?" asked Sarah as she laughed. "Only a few days till you meet with Dave, he finds out that Ed quit, and he releases your soul back to the economy for being the manager everyone quits on."

Alex smirked. "No, I don't think so," he said. "Do you remember Emily? She missed out on the role when we gave it to Ed. She was our number two pick. Well, this is her resume. I just spoke with her, and she is still keen to work here!"

"Amazing!" replied Sarah. "I can't believe your luck!"

"Yeah, I've been thinking about luck, and luck is the problem," said Alex. Sarah looked bemused as Alex continued. "Think back to Nick. We were presented with a great opportunity for him to succeed here. But I didn't prepare well enough to ensure he understood how to do so. There was no real onboarding. You see, luck is when preparation meets opportunity."

Sarah looked at Alex. She didn't respond or say anything as she contemplated his newfound enthusiasm and wisdom.

Without a reaction from Sarah, Alex continued. "So, I've got to be prepared if I'm going to solve this problem once and for all. There are two parts to my preparation. Number one is the what. 'What' means really understanding and documenting what success looks like for Emily at the end of her onboarding, so at that point, I've got a clear way to measure her progress, and I can figure out whether she is a successful fit."

"Like a school report or scorecard?" Sarah replied.

"Exactly," said Alex as he continued. "Number two is the how. 'How' means the plan to help her understand everything necessary for success against that scorecard within ninety days before she becomes a full-time employee. Because for us, that's when her status changes regarding the standard entitlements. This way, if she

Role Scorecard example	
Position	Sales manager
Role purpose	Reporting to the CEO, the sales manager is accountable for effectively leading the sales team to achieve the firm's revenue and gross margin budget
Responsibilities	Lead the sales department in day-to-day people management and ensure team compliance in line with the overall company goals and needs. Hire, coach, train, and hold accountable sales team members to achieve their sales budget individually, thereby contributing to the overall budget. Develop credibility for the sales team function within the business by providing timely and accurate sales insights, analysis of sales trends, sales reports, and sales team trends to support the CEO and other senior executives in making the best decisions in line with company strategy. Be fully responsible for the firm's revenue and gross margin dollar results, including the negative impact of any discounting initiative. Work with the marketing manager to coordinate sales team efforts and maximise marketing spend. Manage all sales recruiting and performance management within the sales team. Regularly develop new initiatives for sales team training and sales team effectiveness on both sales techniques and our products for customers.
Specific measures of success	**Key measure of success:** Gross margin dollars sold per month to budget. Greater than $1.175m per month **Other measures** Revenue: > $2.5m per month by July 2023 Sales team performance: >80% always achieve individual budget Sales team retention: >80% retention per annum Sales pipeline: increase to $50m by October 2023
Competency expectations	**Cultural expectations:** The team expresses pride in working for the sales manager, will rally the sales team to achieve budget when behind, must have a legacy of sales management success, communicate transparently up and down, celebrate wins with the team, and set achievable goals. **Manager's expectations:** Relies on a CRM to achieve results, quick to build trust with team and customers, professional presentation every day, communicates immediately if a customer is thinking about cancelling a contract, any product issues should generate a leadership meeting within three days, and every salesperson follows the documented sales process. **Technical and process expectations:** Proficient in Salesforce, competent in managing out underperforming salespeople, managing customer delivery against manufacturing output, clearly interacting with customers about technical challenges our product solves, and training others on the Quality Assurance system related to the sales team.
Candidate summary	

Figure 6.1 **Role scorecard example**

isn't a successful fit, we know why."

"So how do these work?" enquired Sarah.

"Firstly, we've been building job descriptions all wrong," Alex began. "They are too vague; they don't have measurable accountabilities, which means we're not clear on the expected performance and behaviours." Alex showed Sarah the role scorecard for the sales manager role, as shown in Figure 6.1.

"Here's a role scorecard I've built for Emily's sales manager role that clearly defines what success looks like. It's got the purpose of the role, responsibilities, the way that success is measured—with real targets and dates—and the competency expectations. The competency expectations cover three areas: what she needs to understand about the culture, the technical and process expectations, and my expectations as her manager so that she can succeed in the role."

Sarah read through the role scorecard and commented, "This sure is clear. If Emily can achieve all this, she will be a success. So, what's the second thing, the 'plan for how'?"

"Remember Isabelle from the barbeque?" Alex asked. Sarah nodded in reply. "Well, she said,

'Every new hire has a weekly meeting with their manager during the first ninety days.' And I realized that's the way I get Emily to understand. So, I'm breaking down everything that Emily needs to learn from the role scorecard, and I'm meeting her once weekly for an hour to go through it bit by bit. Here, take a look."

Alex explained the onboarding sprint plan to Sarah that he'd built for Emily, as shown in Figure 6.2. Sarah went through the plan with Alex and finally said, "Well, if Emily's your opportunity, then you're certainly well prepared to enjoy some luck!"

Alex smiled in response and said, "Emily isn't the opportunity. My meeting with Dave is the opportunity. And between the costs that I've found, the role scorecard, and the onboarding sprint plan, I'm well prepared to finally enjoy some luck!" The two laughed as Sarah stood to leave the office.

	Cultural expectations	Manager's expectations	Technical and process expectations
Preboarding	Lunch with the sales team Team member photo uploaded	Visit the office for two hours to answer CEO's questions Watch Salesforce CRM intro video	Complete preboarding forms Read sales process manual Any future leave date requests
Day 1 **Onboarding meeting, Induction, Orientation**	Core values review Behaviours review Two values stories Explain daily huddles and meetings	Company history Company plans and priorities Office plan where everyone sits and their role Review personal professional development goals Verbal commitment to one another Review annual sales budget Critical success factors of the sales team	Review sales material Overview sales team performance Tour production facility with ops manager
Month 1 **Understand**	Core values stories review each week with the manager Review last year's core values award winners Understand BHAG and Brand Promise	Document personal goals and plan Review all sales material and provide a list of weaknesses and improvements needed Weekly meetings with Marketing Manager - understand lead generation and allocation process and weaknesses in the system Meet with all Sales Staff one on one and understand what makes them tick Meet 15 customers	Attend two seminars 12th and 19th June Observe three interviews for new sales staff with CEO Sit in on Sales calls with eight sales staff Attended a sales meeting with four sales staff Proficient in obtaining weekly sales reports from CRM Read Scaling Up book Read HBR article A12 in library

Month 2 Learn & apply	Core values stories review each week with the manager Three core values stories from the sales team Understand BHAG and Brand Promise Daily huddle with sales team embedded Cultural observations report to manager	Review personal goals and plan Implement five sales material improvements Weekly meetings with Marketing Manager - transition to new business projects One sales coaching meeting with every sales team member Meet 20 customers	Attend two seminars 7th and 21st July Participate in five interviews for new sales staff with CEO Sit in on Sales calls with 15 sales staff Attended a sales meeting with six sales staff Read Ultimate sales machine book Read HBR Article A17 in library Build a list of responses to objections with the sales team Two role-play sessions with sales team
Month 3 Embed	Core values stories review each week with the manager Three core values stories from outside the sales team Team building event with sales and marketing teams Five Dysfunctions of a Team cultural report	Review personal goals and plan Implement five sales material improvements Budget recommendations for every sales team member One sales coaching meeting with every sales team member Meet 20 customers Review strategy with CEO	Attend two seminars 14th and 22nd August Run five interviews for new sales staff with CEO Sit in on Sales calls with 15 sales staff Attend a sales meeting with six sales staff Weekly sales reports from CRM to leadership team Read Baseline selling book Read HBR Article A22 in library Expand list of responses to objections Two role play sessions with sales team

Figure 6.2 Onboarding sprint plan example

A few days later, as Alex walked toward Dave's office for his monthly meeting, he thought that without all the work he'd done, he would have been heading in to get fired now. But instead, he knew his numbers, what the problem was, how much it cost, and, importantly for Dave, exactly how to fix it.

Alex went on to spend the next two hours with Dave, even though it was only supposed to be a one-hour meeting. At one point, Dave was shocked as he began to understand how much the ineffective onboarding process was costing the firm. Still, Alex's research and calculations provided the confidence that it was a problem worth investing in. At another point, Alex could feel Dave's simmering rage when he explained how Ed had resigned after only twelve weeks under Alex's watch.

But Dave's rage calmed as Alex explained that Ed's replacement Emily had agreed to join. Then Dave's rage completely subsided when Alex explained that Emily was the first to go through the new role scorecard and Onboarding Sprint Plan. Dave loved that Emily's preboarding had already begun with a team lunch and that Olivia had been assigned as her onboarding buddy. Alex left Dave's office, delighted that he'd finally solved the problem. This was the beginning of the end of the years of mistakes, poor productivity, and resignations, and the real beginning of the team's turnaround.

Just over a month later, Emily joined, and Alex felt her onboarding was progressing well. As he walked back to his office, having just finished a meeting with a new supplier in the boardroom, he almost knocked over Emily on the same corner he and Dave had recently collided.

"Sorry, Alex," said Emily.

"It's okay. I've crashed on this blind corner before. Maybe we need a mirror or something!" Alex replied with a laugh.

Emily smiled. "Oh, by the way, I've been meaning to catch you. Have you got a minute?"

Alex shuddered with horror as he looked down to see Emily holding a piece of paper. "Sure," he said, his voice almost trembling. His mind darted as everything he'd come to believe came into question. As they took the thirty-second walk back to Alex's office, he tried to understand what might have gone wrong. How would he explain it to Dave? Where did he fail? But before he could process these thoughts, they arrived at his office, and Alex instinctively said, "Close the door."

"Umm, okay," replied Emily. She went on, "You know, Alex, I've never started a job where I've learned so much at the beginning and been so clear on what to do. It's like the team here really cares. I just wanted to say thanks and let you know that it hasn't gone unnoticed."

Alex smiled as a sea of relief washed over him. "That's what I'm here for—to help you succeed."

• • •

In developing the accountability side of your business, you must ensure every employee understands exactly what is expected of them and what it takes to succeed in their role, to the point where it is not possible to misunderstand what they must do.

This is the uncomfortable truth that many leaders are reluctant to admit. When I work with leadership teams and determine the people who are not performing, we dig down and ask three key questions:

1 *Are they capable of succeeding in the role?*

2 *Do they understand what it takes to succeed in the role?*

3 *Do they want to succeed in the role?*

We often identify that the employee doesn't fully understand what it takes to succeed in the role. Of the three questions, question number two most speaks to the leader's effectiveness in setting the person up for success. And this was the issue that Sarah identified when she asked Alex these same three questions about Ed leading up to the end of his probation.

It is unfair if a leader doesn't allow employees to succeed because they haven't given them an understanding of how to do so. And yet it is by far the greatest obstacle to building accountability. If people aren't completely clear on how to succeed, it is hypocritical to hold them accountable when they aren't performing as expected.

That's the key to building an effective role scorecard. First, it should make the manager completely clear how an employee will succeed after their onboarding. A separate document called the onboarding sprint plan provides a map of how a new hire will get there.

A new hire might be capable of succeeding in their role, and they might want to succeed in the role. But whether they understand how to succeed in the role is the manager's responsibility through onboarding, and that understanding begins by building a role scorecard.

A manager uses the role scorecard in four separate areas.

1 *In hiring, it paints a clear picture of the type of person you are looking for to fill the role that you can compare against during the hiring process. You can rate each candidate against the criteria within the role scorecard.*

2 *During onboarding, you can clearly explain the expectations and set clear goals.*

3 *After onboarding and when the person has exited probation, you can effectively measure their performance against a scorecard.*

4 *During performance management, you create a clear and specific document before the person starts the role that you can use for robust discussions.*

A manager must build a role scorecard before advertising a vacancy or talking with candidates. The role scorecard will inform you how to write the job advert and provide tips to interview and rate candidates against the criteria set within the role scorecard. You can also share the role scorecard with candidates to clarify expectations during the hiring process. If you're in a larger organization, the role scorecard's completion should probably be a minimum requirement before you are permitted to advertise a vacancy.

The five components of a role scorecard, as previously shown in Figure 6.1, are:

1   *Role Purpose: Outlining in a sentence or two why the job exists and its purpose within the company.*

2   *Responsibilities: The functions, systems, and outputs the role is responsible for.*

3   *Specific measures of success: The results you want to go from A to B by a certain date—for example, sales from $1 million to $1.5 million by the end of 2024.*

4   *Competency expectations: A list of the must-have competencies across three criteria: the culture, managers' expectations, and technical and process expectations. For example, "analysis skills" would be a necessary technical competency for a CFO role, while "risk-taking" would not be required. After each interview, this is used to rate the candidate's competency against the criteria.*

5   *Candidate summary: A list of strengths, areas of concern, and recommendations about each candidate completed at the end of each interview.*

In Figure 6.2, we saw a sample onboarding sprint plan. This plan is built from the role scorecard in Figure 6.1 earlier in this chapter. That role scorecard shows us the overall end goal, and the onboarding sprint plan explains how a new hire will reach the level of competence outlined in the role score-card. Remember that every onboarding sprint plan is different because every candidate is different and in a different situation. They might be 80 percent similar but should be adapted for each individual. You can also download an editable version of this and other tools with a further explanation at my website, evolutionpartners.com.au.

The plan in Figure 6.2 is divided into preboarding, day one, month one, month two, and month three. In each of those times, we're considering the cultural expectations, the managers' expectations, and the technical and process expectations. It's also worth noting the areas where the new hire has achieved sufficient competency, whereby they don't need to work on it any further.

One last tip: the onboarding plan must be achievable in ninety days. One CEO I know set so many learning tasks within the onboarding sprint plan that it might have taken nine months for the new hire to complete them. Perhaps your new hire can only spend twenty hours per week on tasks you set. Ensure your goals are achievable!

The example onboarding sprint plan provided in Figure 6.2 is for a sales manager who controls their time. For a worker who is not in control of their own time, like a worker paid by the hour or by the piece of work completed, the onboarding plan should be different, but the same overall principles apply.

Ideally, your onboarding process should align with the statutory pro-bation period for your country. In other words, you want the onboarding process to enable you to confidently know whether the person should stay or go within the legal probation period. If they must go, it should cost you as little as possible and cause the least damage to your culture while complying with the law. Most countries have a three-to-six-month statutory limit on a probation period, after which standard employment legislation commences.

Of course, you should seek advice from an employment expert in your region, but for the purpose of this book, we're working on ninety days, which is quite common across the world. The rigor of the ninety-day onboarding process I describe in this book will give you absolute confidence about whether you need to exit the person within the legal time frame and begin the hiring process again.

CHAPTER 7

Too Many People Are Leaving

Emily sat in the large meeting room and looked across the table to Alex and Sarah. After ninety days, she felt that she had a good understanding of the role and the company. She believed there weren't any surprises and was confident heading into this meeting to formally conclude her onboarding.

Alex kicked things off. "Hey, Emily, let's get started. We hired you because of who you are. We felt that the values and behaviours you demonstrated during the first interview would make you a successful fit for our team here. You know the story—that Ed had the job and resigned. We can't change that. But we learned from Ed and rebuilt the onboarding process to invest in you so that you can succeed. That's because we believe that you have the raw ingredients to be a great success here, and I think we've proven that over the past three months."

"Well, thanks, Alex," said Emily.

Alex continued, "It's probably no surprise that we're classifying you as a successful fit and want to transition you from probation status to full-time. The feedback from Olivia, your onboarding buddy, has been great, and she agrees that you're a successful fit. In our weekly meetings, you've completed all the tasks and objectives, and frankly, I'm delighted to have you on my team. I now want to give you some specific examples about things you've done well, some of the things you've done that have aligned with our behaviours and core values, and a few opportunities to help you continue to improve."

Over the next hour, Alex and Sarah formally closed out Emily's onboarding by discussing her performance thus far. They reviewed the onboarding sprint plan, the role scorecard, and how it applies to Emily's role moving forward. Finally, they established ongoing reporting for Emily as a part of the team.

•

"This room wasn't built for this," Alex thought as he looked around the large meeting room the entire company had somehow squeezed into. At least a dozen people needed to stand because there wasn't room for any more chairs.

Alex walked to the centre and said to the group, "Let's get started, everyone." He paused as the chatter subsided. "Too many people are leaving. And even worse, most of them are leaving in the first year. I know you might look to me and think that many of those who left were in my team, which is why I took on the job to sort out this problem."

At his monthly meeting with Dave a few weeks earlier, Dave had been so impressed with the new onboarding process Alex had run with Emily that Dave asked Alex to present it to the whole firm at an all-hands meeting.

Alex had now gained the room's full attention. He continued, "Dave said something to me a few months ago, and it really started me on this journey. He said, *'If you don't know what you're doing to them that's making them leave, what are we paying you for?'*." Alex looked over to Dave, who didn't seem too happy that he was being quoted. "But Dave, you were right!"

Dave jumped in. "You seem surprised?" he asked with a smile. A subtle laugh could be heard across the crowd.

"Anyway," Alex continued, "We don't know why people are staying or leaving because we don't know if people are a successful or unsuccessful fit in the role they're hired into. Basically, we've been hiring people and relying on them to draw on their previous experience and hoping they will work it out themselves. I think it's fair to say that over many years, we've proven that this doesn't work. Because, like I said, too many people are leaving, and it hurts every one of us in this room."

"We've put together some ballpark estimates on what this is costing us, in hard dollar costs, productivity, and the opportunity to improve our retention. And so armed with that, we set about building a new onboarding process for new hires, which we trialled with Emily." Alex looked at Emily and asked, "Emily, any feedback for the group?"

Sheepishly, Emily stood up and said, "I definitely understand how to succeed." She paused as she considered her next words. "I knew what was expected of me, and with my weekly onboarding meetings with Alex and my buddy Olivia, I felt like you really cared. It's definitely the best onboarding that I've ever had."

"Thanks, Emily," Alex said as he turned to the crowd. "I now want to show you the timeline we use for onboarding and what each part means." Alex clicked his laptop to advance the slide deck and displayed the onboarding process timeline in Figure 7.1.

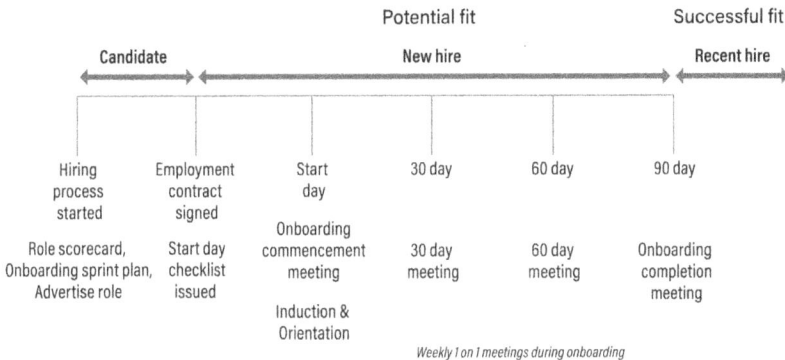

Figure 7.1 **Onboarding process timeline**

Alex started by explaining the definition of onboarding.

"Onboarding is not hiring. It's not induction. It's not orientation, and it's not training.

Onboarding is the process of taking someone from outside our organization and making them a productive, independent, and confident member of our team who understands the culture, the technical and process expectations, and their manager's expectations. The onboarding period begins when a person has signed an employment contract and ends when they are a useful, valuable team member.

Before they sign the contract, a person is a candidate. After that, they are a potential fit. That means they can potentially fit in here, but we need to validate that during the onboarding. Finally, they are a successful fit only after they have completed the thirteen weekly onboarding meetings with their direct manager. And that's important. It's not Sarah in HR's job; the manager owns the onboarding."

Alex continued, "The problem is that we've been doing an induction and an orientation, but we haven't been onboarding new hires."

Alex clicked to advance to the next slide, which explained the different processes adjacent to onboarding as shown below.

Induction is where you admit a new employee to an organization or role. It's like a license to operate; it provides the employee the ability to participate in the organization. You might classify a new hire as having been inducted when they have completed the forms to get paid and pay taxes, know their computer login and how to access their email, and have been issued security access cards.

Orientation is the process of helping a person become familiar with a location or situation. It is how they come to know their way around. After a new hire has completed orientation, they should know the location of the IT and HR departments and who to talk with if they need help. They should also know emergency procedures and the locations of the exits and restrooms. Orientation might also include things like car parking arrangements or an explanation of the org chart and who does what.

Training is where you teach an employee a new skill or behaviour or help them to improve an existing one. Training applies both to existing employees and new hires during the onboarding process. Once trained on a subject, new hires within the onboarding process should understand the processes and systems required to do their job. Or, to put it another way, they should understand "the way we do things here."

•

"Because we haven't been doing a good job onboarding new hires, there's been a difference between what new hires know and what they should know. Therefore, people have been doing things the way they think is right, doing things they shouldn't, or neglecting to do the things they should. All these things add up, creating more errors, issues, rework, and lower productivity. It's like there's a debt that we carry and continually service because we haven't onboarded these people well."

Alex clicked on the next slide, shown in Figure 7.2.

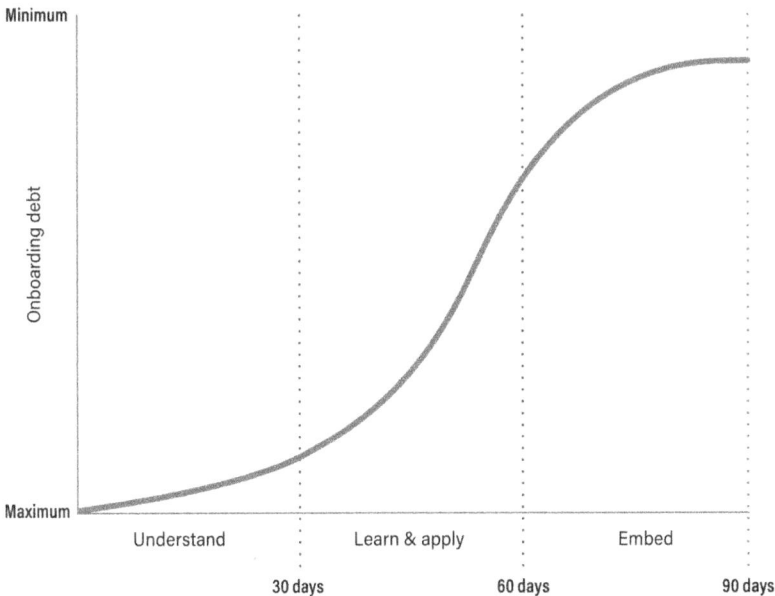

Figure 7.2 The three stages of onboarding

"So across each of the three months for a new hire's onboarding, we want to reduce this debt. But it doesn't happen evenly. In the first month, our new hire is in the understand stage. Everything is new, and they are understanding their role at each of the four weekly meetings. In the second stage, they are learning and applying on the job, which is where the greatest onboarding debt reduction occurs. Then finally, in the third month, we are embedding what they have understood, learned, and applied."

"Can you give us an example?" asked Olivia from the crowd.

"Sure, let's use Emily," said Alex.

"In her first month, the understand stage, Emily attended sales meetings as an observer alongside other salespeople. Then in month two, during the learn and apply stage, she attended and ran sales meetings with another salesperson attending as an observer. In the third month, Emily attended sales meetings alone and provided detailed updates to me after each meeting. Remember that Emily was also unlearning things from her previous jobs, which was an important part of learning how we do things here."

A question came from Ramesh at the front of the room. "Why is our onboarding so bad? Why has it become such a problem?"

"Thanks, Ramesh," Alex replied. "Onboarding is a once-in-a-while process without a clear owner. We know who is accountable for sales. We know who is accountable for ordering supplies and who pays the supplier invoices. And we're clear about who is accountable for resolving computer issues. And by accountable, I mean they will probably be fired if they consistently do an inadequate job."

Dave nodded his head enthusiastically.

"We even know who is accountable for hiring. Sarah brings in pre-qualified candidates, but managers interview and decide. But hiring has a very clear outcome: to fill a role. If the position is filled, the job is done. People then move on and get back to work. Sure, hiring is a part-time distraction from a person's day-to-day role, but there is a clear success metric. Vacancy filled. We then move on and get back to work."

"The thing is," Alex continued as he clicked his computer, revealing the image shown in Figure 7.3, "that onboarding is perhaps the only key process without a clear owner that needs to be performed by the entire organization.

If someone does a bad job of onboarding, there's probably no chance they will be fired. Onboarding doesn't contribute to a clear objective like other processes, where we might get more sales or faster project completion. And onboarding is part-time. A busy manager might only perform an onboarding process once every three or six months."

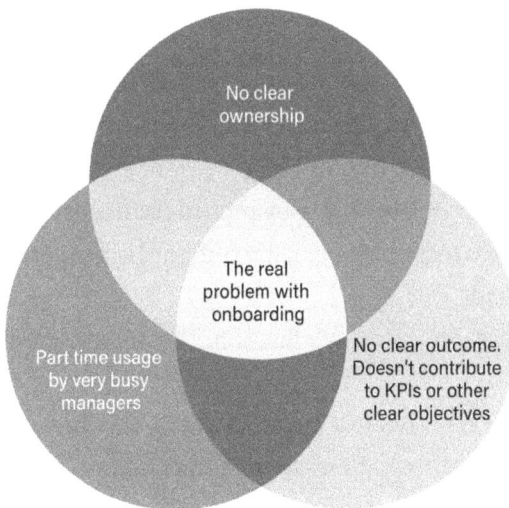

Figure 7.3 The real problem with onboarding

A voice came from the back of the room. It was Dan, who always loved to ask a challenging question. "Alex, how about Phil? He was never going to work, maybe anywhere!"

The crowd erupted with laughter before Dan continued. "No number of meetings would get him to work out here. He was just a bad fit. How would your meetings handle another Phil?"

"We all know Phil's aversion to work," Alex replied, "but here's the thing. We want this process to validate whether the person we hired is a successful fit and should stay or an unsuccessful fit and should exit. Take a look at my next slide."

Alex moved to the slide shown in Figure 7.4. "This is the point easy concept. Not long after Phil joined, we knew his actual performance was lower than our intended performance. That's when it was easy for us, or me, to talk with him about it. But I didn't, so time went on, and Phil's performance didn't improve, but our expectations for him to improve his performance continued to grow, as we'd expect with anybody new. The gap got bigger, and the situation got to point difficult. It got challenging to act on that performance gap because I hadn't acted at point easy.

Of course, because I didn't act at point difficult, our performance expectations continued to grow, and Phil's performance actually declined. Things then got to point crisis where everybody knew that something had to be done. The relevance of point easy, Dan, is that with a clear role scorecard and weekly onboarding meetings, we never get to point difficult."

Dan nodded as if to acknowledge that the answer addressed his concern.

Alex spent the next twenty minutes answering further questions from the team and talking about scorecards and the onboarding sprint plan. As Alex closed the meeting, Dave thanked him for his efforts to fix the problems they had suffered for so long. The room slowly emptied, and Sarah helped Alex rearrange chairs and clean up.

"You know," said Sarah, "that was pretty impressive. Not just today, I mean the whole thing, since Dave told you to start preparing to present the hiring costs and challenges to him. You just turned our biggest problem into a great opportunity for us all."

Alex laughed out loud. "Ha, I only got lucky," he replied. "Remember, luck is when preparation meets opportunity."

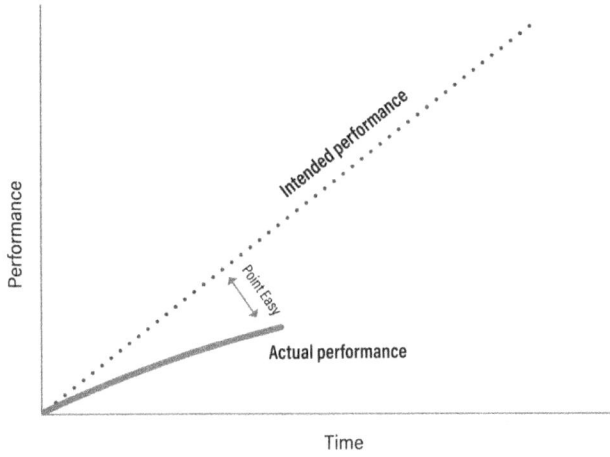

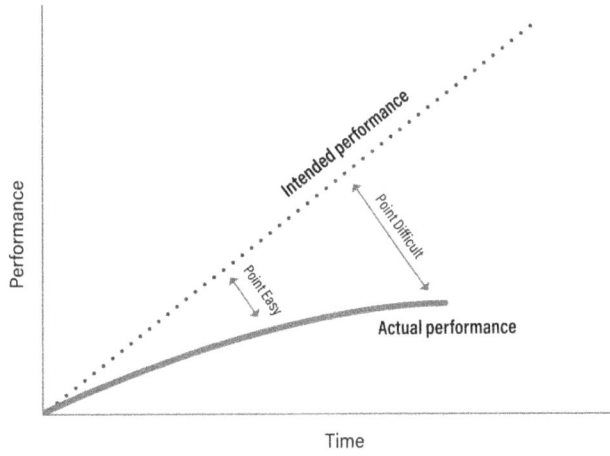

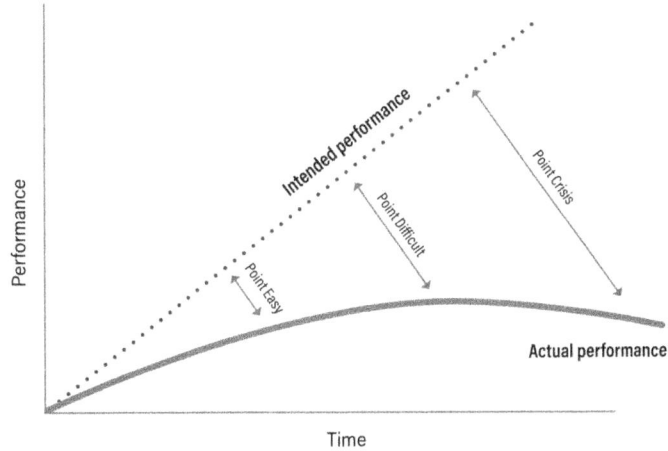

Figure 7.4 **Point easy concept**

• • •

You might recall from Chapter 2 the graph reproduced in Figure 7.5 demonstrating that the longer an onboarding process, the greater a new hire's understanding. In my research, I also asked respondents about the length of their onboarding processes.

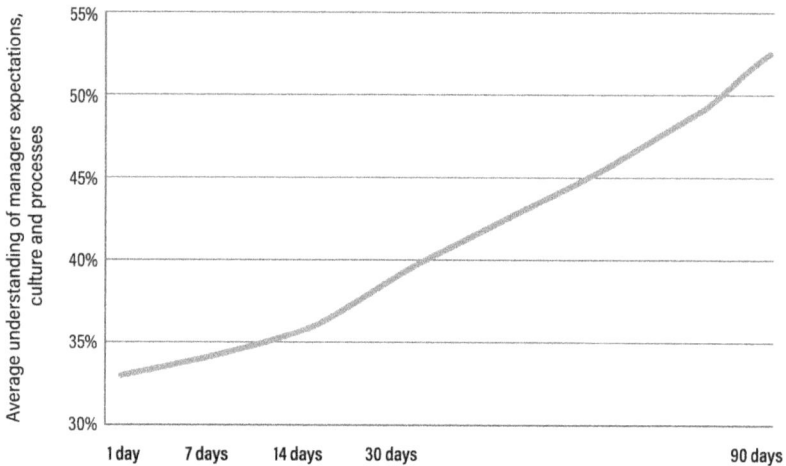

Figure 7.5 **Longer onboarding leads to a better understanding of expectations and processes**

When we overlay the responses from that question about onboarding duration onto the question about understanding from Figure 7.5, as shown in Figure 7.6, we see that 83 percent of recent hires undergo an onboarding process of fourteen days or less. Yet, the new hire's understanding of the manager's expectations, the culture, and the company processes only begins to improve at thirty days and continues to improve through to ninety days.

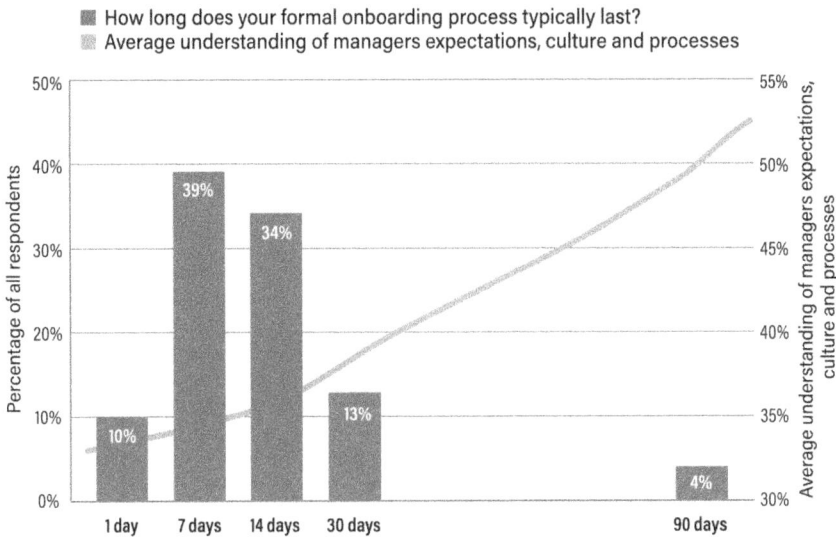

How long does your formal onboarding process typically last?
Average understanding of managers expectations, culture and processes

Figure 7.6 Recent hire understanding compared to the percentage
of total onboarding time for all respondents

This graph is a powerful indictment of the current global process of onboarding. Most respondents to my survey had a seven-day onboarding process—yet the real impact of onboarding begins to accelerate after thirty days. If employees' onboardings do not progress past thirty days – and it's clear from my research that most don't—they are missing the opportunity to become fully effective in their roles.

Their managers, and the organizations they belong to, can't possibly expect to have teams with a healthy and productive culture. This is why Nick and Ed ended up resigning. They had not been made to feel that they were valued members of the team—let alone understand the crucial aspects of their roles in the company.

Implementing a ninety-day onboarding process should be a priority for you and your organization. Let's say your competitors have a seven-or-fourteen-day onboarding process – as illustrated in Figure 7.6—yet the real impact of onboarding begins to accelerate after thirty days through to ninety days. Could this create a strategic advantage for you? If your employees' understanding is significantly higher than your competitors' employees, how would your firm differ from competitors after a few years and perhaps tens or hundreds of hires? This gap also impacts other existing workers in the firm. If not taught during onboarding, there are so many things that your recent hires will never understand, and you will never find the time to teach them. Most managers act as if their employees might absorb key concepts via osmosis.

This is the terrible ongoing legacy of onboarding debt.

But it doesn't need to be this way. This book aims to empower you, the reader, to answer the following question.

"How can we reduce onboarding debt and make new hires more effective, faster?"

I hope that I've given you the tools to reduce your onboarding debt, and make new hires more effective, faster.

Next Steps

Thank you for reading *Onboarded for Managers*.

My primary objective in writing this book was to address what I view as the most significant opportunity in leadership today, which carries an enormous cost. I then wanted to take that opportunity and provide you with a simple, practical, and actionable tool you can immediately implement into your firm to produce a significant impact.

Onboarded for Managers is intended to be a short, easy-to-read guide so that team members can understand how and why to implement the principles and tools from the book *Onboarded*. Managers can only implement successful onboarding if they understand why it's worth their effort. *Onboarded* explains the concepts and tools in this book in greater detail and contains more information about my research study and other research in the field.

As I noted in Chapter 7, for most readers, the most significant hurdle they will face in implementing this process is that onboarding has no clear ownership or outcome and is a part-time process. These are not insignificant challenges. As a business community, we haven't reached the point where it is so rare to find effective onboarding without good reason, even though it is very expensive if done poorly.

And as I've demonstrated throughout this book, the cost of not applying a simple process, owned by the direct manager of a new hire, can be outrageous.

Your journey needn't be as difficult as Alex's. We're here to help. You can download an editable version of the tools in this book at my website: evolutionpartners.com.au where we you will also find explainers and a short video course about Onboarded and how to use the tools.

If you need further help implementing these tools, my firm, Evolution Partners, will be able to assist you, or we can introduce you to some of our certified coaching partners across the globe. You can find me at *brad.giles@ evolutionpartners.com.au*, where I'd love to hear from you.